1 What are microbes?

Microbes are invisible to us. They are very small. They are measured in 0.001 mm (1/1000 mm). Microbes can only be seen with very powerful microscopes. Microbes include single-celled plants and animals. The most important are **fungi**, **bacteria** and **viruses**. Microbes that cause disease are sometimes called 'germs'. Not all microbes are dangerous. Some are very useful to us.

M

100 + Fungi

10 million Viruses

1000 + Bacteria

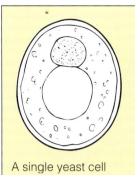

A single yeast cell — 0.005 mm

Fungi may live as single cells. Usually these join to form threads. Fungi feed on dead and decaying plants and animals, or on living cells.

Yeast cells seen under the electron microscope × 6000

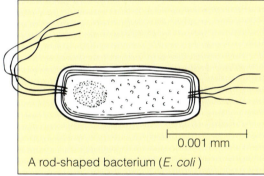

A rod-shaped bacterium (*E. coli*) — 0.001 mm

Bacteria live as single cells. They have different shapes. Bacteria absorb food from wherever they are living. Their wastes can be harmful to us.

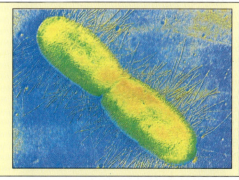

A single *E. coli* bacterium seen under the electron microscope × 13500

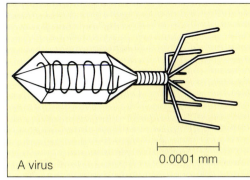

A virus — 0.0001 mm

Viruses are not really alive. They do not feed or breathe. They can not survive alone. To multiply and survive they must enter living cells. So they are always harmful and difficult to study.

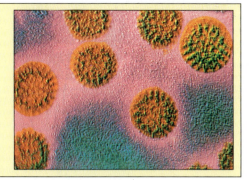

Rotaviruses seen under the electron microscope × 20 600

Q1 What are microbes?

Q2 Are all microbes useful to humans?

Q3 Which are the largest microbes?

Q4 Which microbes need the greatest magnification to be seen?

Extension exercise 1 can be used now.

1 What are microbes?

Safety in the laboratory

Microbes are so small that we need very powerful microscopes to see them. We can study microbes by giving them ideal living conditions. Then they can grow and multiply. They will make large groups of microbes called **colonies**. These are big enough to see.

Some microbes are harmful and cause disease. To be safe our experiments must be done with great care. Your teacher will show you the **sterile** techniques. Listen carefully to the explanation of the safety points. You need to understand these when you do your practical work.

Apparatus

- ☐ culture of *E. coli*
- ☐ 2 Petri dishes of nutrient agar
- ☐ marker pen ☐ inoculating loop
- ☐ Bunsen burner ☐ sticky tape
- ☐ eye protection

 Biohazard – a sterile technique must be used **at all times**.

A Sterile preparation
Each **Petri dish** has been prepared in sterile (microbe-free) conditions. Each contains a special food called **agar jelly**. The lids have been kept on. ▲

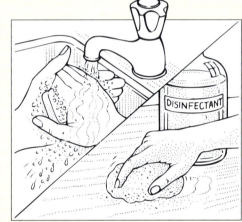

B Sterile technique at the start of every lesson ▲
1 Wash your hands.
2 Swab the bench with disinfectant.

C Labelling Petri dishes
Write your name, the date and dish number neatly on the bottom of both dishes. ▲

D Flaming a loop
Heat the **inoculating loop** in the flame until it glows red. ▲

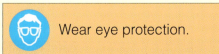 Wear eye protection.

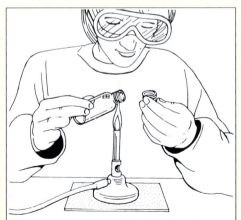

E Flaming a bottle
Unscrew the bottle of microbes. Hold the cap. Hold the bottle in a medium flame for 2–3 seconds. ▲

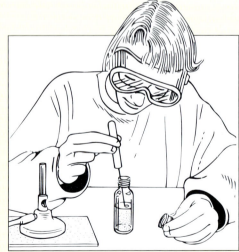

F Inoculating a loop
Dip the flamed loop into the microbes.
Quickly replace the cap. ▲

1 What are microbes?

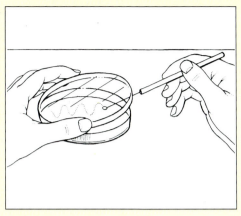

G **Streaking a plate**
Lift the lid of dish 1 as little as possible. Streak the loop on the agar. Quickly replace the lid. ▲

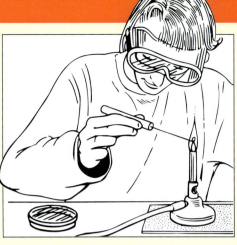

H **Flaming a used loop**
Put the loop into the flame slowly. (Don't let it splutter.) Now streak dish 2 as before. ▲

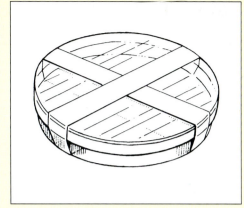

I **Securing a dish lid**
Secure the dish lids with tape but do not seal. ▲

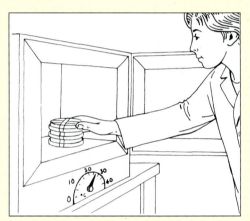

J **Incubating a dish**
Store the dishes upside down in an **incubator** at 25–30°C for 2–3 days. ▲

K **Sterile technique at the end of every lesson**
Clear away the apparatus. Swab the bench with disinfectant. Wash your hands. ▲

L **Looking at the results**
Never open the Petri dishes. Look at the microbes through the lid of the dish. ▲

 Do not open the Petri dishes. Look at the microbes through the top of the plate.

Q1 What does sterile mean?

Q2 Draw the dishes as shown. Complete them to show what they looked like after incubation.

Dish 1. Loop from microbes   Dish 2. Flamed loop

Q3 Which dish had the most microbes?

Q4 Were there any microbes on the loop after it was flamed?

Q5 Do you think that there were any microbes on the loop at the start?

Q6 Why were the dishes sealed?

Q7 Why should you never open the lid of a dish after incubation?

Q8 Why should you always wash your hands at the end of practical work?

1 What are microbes?

Safety in the laboratory

Let's see if you remember all the safety points from the demonstration. The students in the picture didn't understand how important it was to be careful! Many were ill after their practical lesson!

Q1 Copy this table.

Mistake	Why is it dangerous?

Q2 Look carefully at the picture. List each mistake that you can see. Write down why it is dangerous.

Q3 Design a safety poster for your laboratory. Make it bright and colourful with a clear safety message.

1 What are microbes?

Where can we find microbes?

Try and find some microbes. Collect some samples from different places.

Q1 Copy this table.

Dish number	Place sampled	Appearance after incubation
1	Open to air	
2	Sealed	
3		
4		
5		

Apparatus

- ☐ 6 Petri dishes of agar
- ☐ marker pen ☐ sticky tape
- ☐ disinfectant
- ☐ 4 cotton buds in sterile water

 Biohazard – a sterile technique must be used **at all times**.

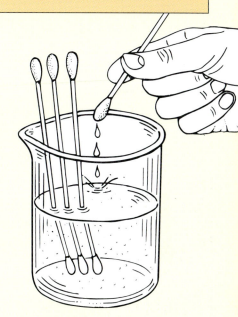

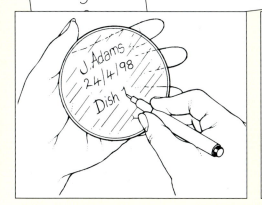

bench
floor
coin
door handle
soap

A Label the bottom of all dishes with your name, date and dish number. Leave dish 1 with the agar open to the air. Seal dish 2. ▲

B Some places are dangerous to sample without special precautions. Those on the list are safer, but care is still needed. Choose four of the places. Record them in the table. ▲

C Take a cotton bud. Remove the excess water. Wipe it on the surface of place 3. ▲

Q2 Which sample do you think grew the most microbes?

Q3 How many different types of growth can you see in each sample?

Q4 What was the purpose of the **control** (the sealed dish 2)?

Q5 Some places would be dangerous to sample because there would be germs present. Copy this table and complete it with your ideas.

Safe places	Unsafe places

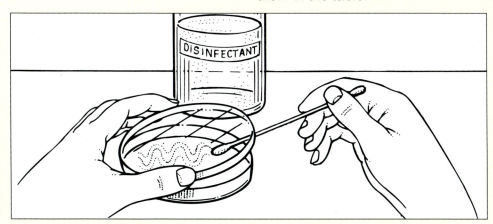

D Lift the lid of dish 3 as little as possible. Streak the surface 3 times. Replace the lid. Put the used cotton bud in the disinfectant. Repeat **C–D** for places 4, 5, and 6. Then secure all the dish lids. Incubate your dishes at 25–30°C for 2–3 days. Look at your results and complete the table. ▲

 Do not open the Petri dishes. Look at the microbes through the top of the plate.

1 What are microbes?

Why do we need to culture microbes?

A single microbe is invisible to us. When we incubate the dishes the bacteria reproduce **asexually**. They divide themselves into two genetically identical individuals (**clones**). Soon colonies (large groups of thousands of bacteria) are formed, which are large enough to see.

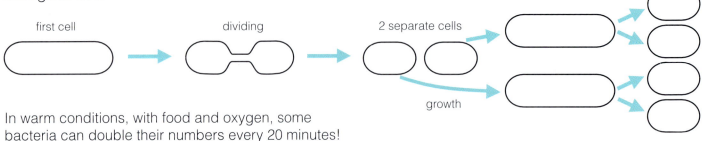

In warm conditions, with food and oxygen, some bacteria can double their numbers every 20 minutes!

Q1 Copy this table.
Use a calculator to help you work out the numbers to complete the table.

Time	0	20 min	40 min	1 hour	1h 20 min	1h 40 min	2h	2h 20 min	2h 40 min	3h
Number of bacteria	1	2	4							

Q2 Draw a graph as shown. Plot the numbers of bacteria for each hour with a cross. Join the crosses with a smooth curve. Write a title on your graph.

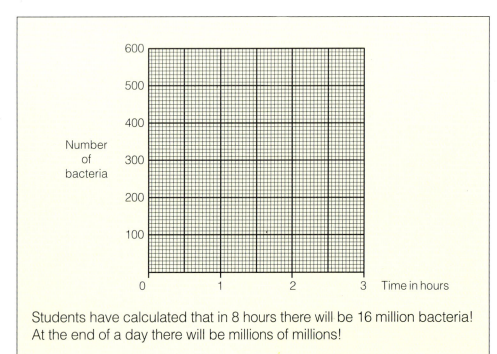

Students have calculated that in 8 hours there will be 16 million bacteria! At the end of a day there will be millions of millions!

Q3 What do bacteria do when we incubate them?

Q4 What are ideal conditions for bacteria?

Q5 How would you describe the rate at which bacteria reproduce?

Q6 Is it possible to draw a graph to show the numbers of bacteria after five hours? Explain your answer.

Q7 A fly lands on a cream cake. It leaves one disease-causing microbe behind. You don't know this. You buy the cake on the way to school. Eight hours later you eat the cake for tea. What may happen?

Q8 Why should you never take the lid off a dish after incubation?

1 What are microbes?

What conditions do microbes need?

Microbes are living organisms. They need food, water and usually oxygen. We give them water and food in the nutrient agar. The way we seal the Petri dish lets air in. See if you can find out what happens to microbes at different temperatures.

Q1 Copy this table.

Dish	Place	Temperature	Appearance after 2–3 days
1	Fridge	5°C	
2	Room	20°C	
3	Incubator	30°C	

Apparatus

- ☐ 3 Petri dishes of agar
- ☐ marker pen ☐ sticky tape
- ☐ Bunsen burner
- ☐ inoculating loop
- ☐ eye protection
- ☐ **culture** of microbes
- ☐ 0–100°C thermometer

 Biohazard – a sterile technique must be used **at all times**.

 Wear eye protection when sterilising the loop.

A Label the bottom of each dish with your name, date and dish number. ▲

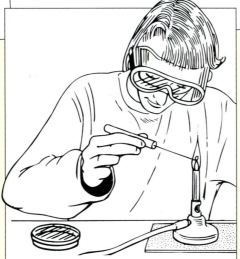

B Flame the loop. Flame the bottle of microbes. ▲

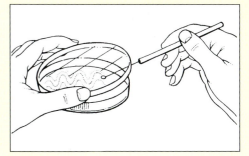

C Dip the flamed loop into the microbes. Lift the lid of dish 1 as little as possible. Streak the agar three times. Quickly close the lid. ▲

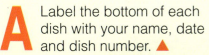 Do not open the Petri dishes. Look at the microbes through the top of the plate.

D Repeat **B** and **C** for dishes 2 and 3. Secure all the dish lids. Keep each dish at the right temperature for 2–3 days. Look at your results. Complete your table. ▲

Q2 What do microbes need to stay alive?

Q3 At which temperature did the most microbes grow?

Q4 At which temperature did the least microbes grow?

Q5 You buy a cream cake early in the morning. Unknown to you a fly has been on it. Where should you keep the cake until tea time?

Cutout sheet 1 can be used now.

2 Microbes and health

How do we get infections?

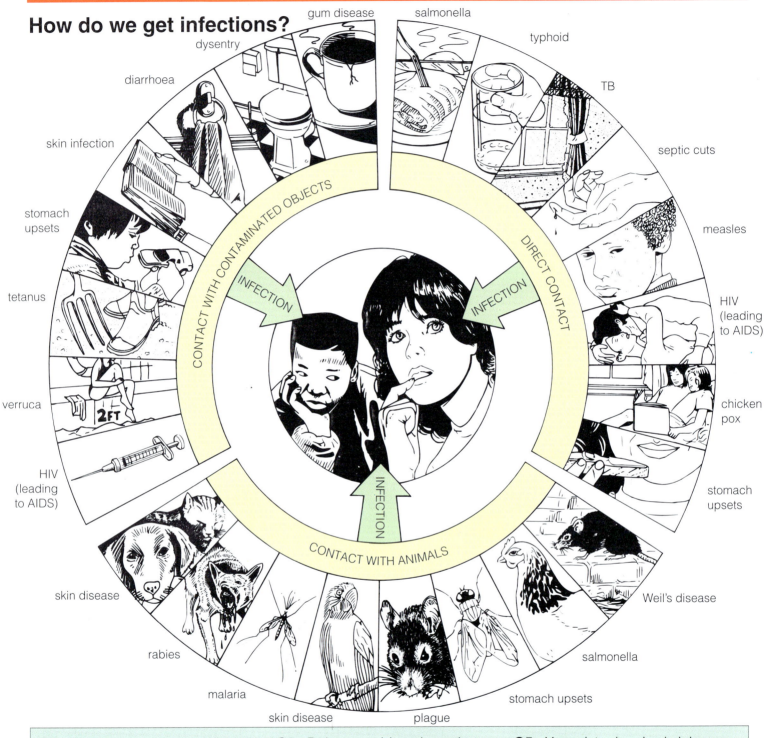

Q1 Barry has a verruca. Where could he have got it from?

Q2 Why should you not drink from cracked cups?

Q3 Delroy was bitten by a dog. Which disease could he get?

Q4 Your mum has a septic finger. Is it safe for her to make your sandwiches? Explain your answer.

Q5 Your sister has had sickness and diarrhoea for 3 days. What care should the rest of the family take to avoid getting the infection?

Q6 Why should you always wash your hands after handling pets?

2 Microbes and health

Why aren't we ill more often?

We are surrounded by disease-causing microbes, or germs. They try to attack us and cause infection. Yet we are not ill very often. We are protected by our body's defence mechanisms.

MICROBES CAN'T GET IN...

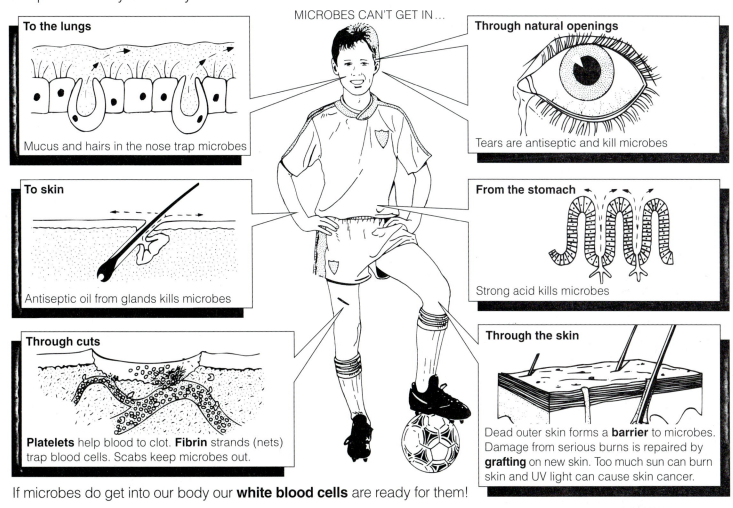

To the lungs — Mucus and hairs in the nose trap microbes

Through natural openings — Tears are antiseptic and kill microbes

To skin — Antiseptic oil from glands kills microbes

From the stomach — Strong acid kills microbes

Through cuts — **Platelets** help blood to clot. **Fibrin** strands (nets) trap blood cells. Scabs keep microbes out.

Through the skin — Dead outer skin forms a **barrier** to microbes. Damage from serious burns is repaired by **grafting** on new skin. Too much sun can burn skin and UV light can cause skin cancer.

If microbes do get into our body our **white blood cells** are ready for them!

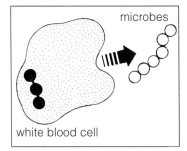
white blood cell — microbes

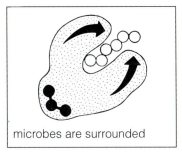
microbes are surrounded

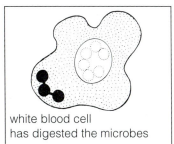
white blood cell has digested the microbes

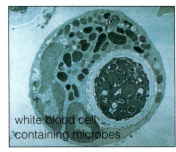
white blood cell containing microbes

Q1 What can microbes do to us?

Q2 Why aren't we ill more often?

Q3 A germ lands on your skin. Why will it be unlikely to cause an infection?

Q4 Yuk Ling ate a cake. She did not know that a fly had been on it. Why wasn't she ill?

Q5 David cut his arm when he fell off his bike. Why didn't his cut get infected?

Q6 Our defence mechanisms are good. Nurse Smith is in contact with a lot of microbes. Some may get into her body. What will happen to these microbes?

2 Microbes and health

Are there microbes on our hands?

See if you can find out how clean your hands are!

Q1 Copy this table.

Dish	Appearance after a few days
1	
2	

Apparatus
- ☐ 2 dishes of agar ☐ sticky tape
- ☐ marker pen ☐ warm water
- ☐ soap ☐ nail brush
- ☐ paper towels

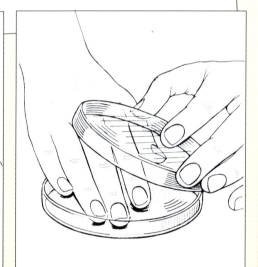
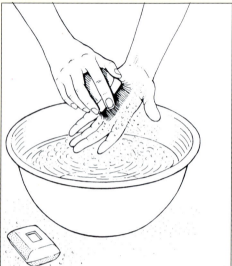

A Label the bottom of both dishes with your name, date and dish number. ▲

B Lift the lid off dish 1. Gently press your fingers on to the agar (enough to leave an impression but not enough to damage the agar). Replace the lid. ▲

C Wash your hands thoroughly. Dry them. Repeat **B** with dish 2. Secure the lids. Incubate the dishes at 25–30°C for 2–3 days. Then record your results in your table. ▲

Microbes and dirt can be trapped in stale sweat and oil, blocking pores. Regular washing usually prevents problems. Infections like spots and **acne** can occur even on clean skin. Squeezing spots spreads the infection. Antibiotics may be needed.

 Do not open the Petri dishes. Look at the microbes through the top of the plate.

Q2 Which dish had the least growth of microbes?

Q3 Can microbes live on our hands?

Q4 Does washing your hands in warm, soapy water remove any microbes?

Q5 Were the microbes doing any harm to your hands?

Q6 Do you think that your hands could pass microbes from one place to another?

Q7 Copy and complete this table.

Washing your hands is important	
Before...	After...

2 Microbes and health

What happens to us if we get an infection?

Many microbes live harmlessly on us. We have got used to them and stay well. Other microbes, or germs, can make us ill.

Infection occurs when germs enter the body. Germs find ideal conditions and multiply rapidly. Levels of their poisonous waste products increase.

The incubation time

Different diseases have different incubation times. For example, it takes three days before you know you have a cold, 2–3 weeks for chicken pox and some years for AIDS.

During this time your body contains microbes but you don't have any symptoms. However, you can infect other people.

After the incubation time **symptoms**, or signs, of the disease appear.

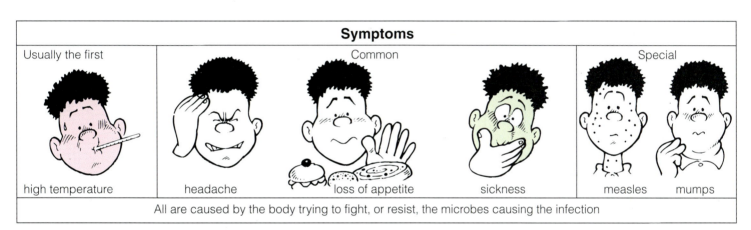

Symptoms

Usually the first: high temperature

Common: headache, loss of appetite, sickness

Special: measles, mumps

All are caused by the body trying to fight, or resist, the microbes causing the infection

Q1 What makes us ill?

Q2 What is the first symptom of most diseases?

Q3 Microbes have entered John's body. He has no symptoms. Can he infect anyone else?

Q4 What are the symptoms of a cold?

Q5 What was the highest Sue's temperature reached?

Q6 How could Sue stop her cold from spreading?

Q7 For how long do you think that Sue felt really ill?

Q8 On which day was Sue's temperature back to normal?

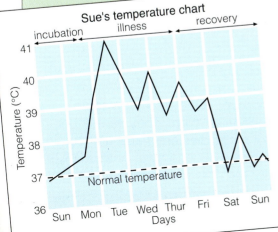

2 Microbes and health

What is immunity?

We don't always get a disease, even if people around us are ill. We are **immune**. Our white blood cells give us **resistance** to the disease. They help us to fight infection in two ways.

1 **Toxins** (the poisonous wastes) from microbes cause disease symptoms. White blood cells make chemicals called **antitoxins** to destroy these poisons.

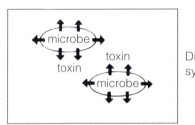

2 White blood cells also make **antibodies**. There is a different antibody for each type of microbe. Antibodies make microbes stick together. Then microbes can't move around the body. Other white blood cells can then attack and destroy microbes more easily.

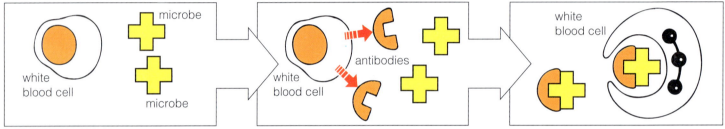

Babies are born with some immunity. They get antibodies from their mother. This immunity doesn't last long. As we grow up we meet lots of new microbes. We get many diseases in childhood. Usually we are immune as adults.

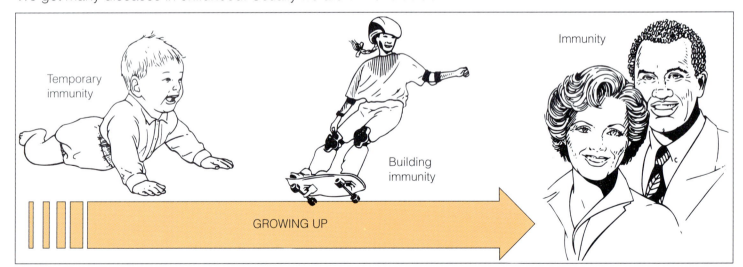

Infection with a new microbe causes antibody production. This is a slow process. Microbes multiply. Then disease symptoms appear. We are ill. When there are enough antibodies we recover. If they meet the same microbes again our white blood cells 'recognise' them. They 'remember' how to make the right antibodies. Lots of antibodies are made quickly. So we do not usually get diseases like measles a second time. Antibodies that we make ourselves give us protection for life. This is **natural immunity**.

Extension exercise 2 can be used now.

2 Microbes and health

▶ Some microbes are dangerous. They can cause permanent damage or kill us before we have had time to make antibodies. Our bodies need help. We need artificial protection. Millions of lives have been saved by **vaccinations**. Vaccines are weak forms of microbes or their toxins. They are injected into the blood or swallowed. Then we make antibodies. We then have a lifetime protection from the dangerous microbes.

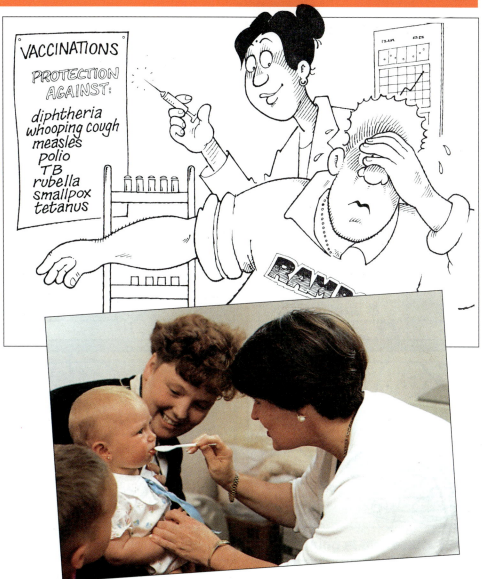

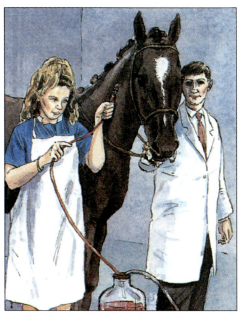

▲ Some dangerous microbes do not have a weak form. Vaccines cannot be made. People need protection quickly if there is an outbreak of a dangerous disease. Then we are injected with ready-made antibodies or antitoxins. These have been made in the body of another person or animal. Antibodies that we have not made for ourselves don't last long. We need a 'booster' or second injection to have enough antibodies for protection.

Extension exercise 3 can be used now.

Q1 Why are babies immune to the common diseases?

Q2 Which cells give us resistance to disease?

Q3 Janet had chicken pox when she was seven years old. Now her brother Peter has the disease. Why won't Janet become ill?

Q4 How can we be given immunity artificially?

Q5 Copy this table and see if you can complete it. You may need to ask your parents, friends or teacher for help. Or you could use a textbook.

Disease	Age for vaccination

2 Microbes and health

What are the common diseases?

The most common diseases are caught easily. They are easily passed on.

▶ **Fungi**

We do not suffer from many fungal diseases. Ringworm and thrush are diseases caused by fungi. The athlete's foot fungus likes the warmth and sweat between toes. It causes itching. This is irritating but does not seriously harm us.

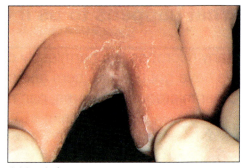
Athlete's foot

▶ **Bacteria**

Bacteria cause boils, sore throats, typhoid, tetanus, cholera, TB, diptheria, pneumonia, salmonella food poisoning, impetigo and whooping cough. Some bacteria can cause death.

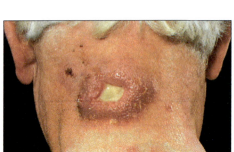
A boil

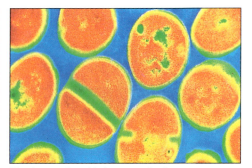
The bacteria which cause boils

▶ **Viruses**

Viruses cause colds, 'flu and verrucae. People usually get better quickly. They also cause mumps and chicken pox which make us ill for longer. Some viral diseases can cause permanent damage, e.g. polio. Measles can cause blindness and deafness. German measles (rubella) can affect unborn babies in the same way. Viral diseases like AIDS and rabies can cause death.

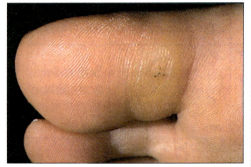
A verruca

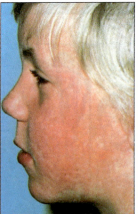
A measles victim

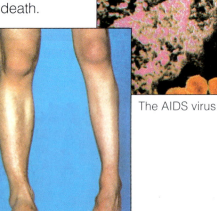
A polio victim

The AIDS virus

The rabies virus

Q1 Copy this table of typical childhood diseases.

Disease	Tally
Athlete's foot	
Boils	
Chicken pox	
'Flu and colds	
German measles	
Measles	
Mumps	
Sore throat	
Verruca	
Whooping cough	

Ask each student in your group which diseases they have had. Record their answers by keeping a tally count.

Tally

I=1, II=2, III=3, IIII=4, IIII=5, IIII I=6, IIII II=7, IIII III=8, etc

Q2 Draw a bar graph to represent your class results.

Q3 Which are the most common diseases?

Q4 Why do you think these diseases are so common?

2 Microbes and health

Can microbes live on our food?

You are going to prepare some samples of food to see if microbes can live on them.

Apparatus

- ☐ 5 screw top containers or jam jars ☐ marker pen ☐ knife
- ☐ 5 white tiles ☐ dropper
- ☐ beaker of water
- ☐ samples of bread, tomato, jam, cheese, orange peel

Q1 Copy this table.

Food	Appearance when fresh	Appearance after 1 week
Cheese		

 Biohazard – a sterile technique must be used **at all times**.

 Do not taste food samples

A Take one sample and cut it into four pieces on a tile. Complete the first two columns of the table. Repeat these steps, using a separate tile for each food sample.

B Use a dropper to moisten the food on each tile. Leave them uncovered for a day. ▼

C Next day check that the food is moist. Cover and label each food. Leave the samples in a warm place for a week. Do not uncover the food but look at it carefully. Complete the last column of the table. ◀

 Do not open the containers. Look at the microbes through the glass.

Q2 Which food had changed the most?

Q3 Mould is caused by microbes. How many types of mould can you see?

Q4 Describe the sort of growths that you can see.

Q5 Where do you think that the moulds have come from?

Q6 Why do you think that you are not allowed to use meat for this experiment?

Extension exercise 4 can be used now.

2 Mirobes and health

What does bread mould (*Mucor*) look like?

Let's have a look at the fungus which grows on bread.

Apparatus

- ☐ microscope ☐ lamp
- ☐ dropper ☐ forceps
- ☐ mounted needle
- ☐ glass slide and coverslip
- ☐ *Mucor* culture in a dish
- ☐ small beaker of water
- ☐ eye protection

Biohazard – a sterile technique must be used **at all times**.

A Do not open the dish. Look carefully at the mould. Then set up the microscope on low power. Move the mirror until there is good light. Turn the focusing knob as far as possible as shown. ▼

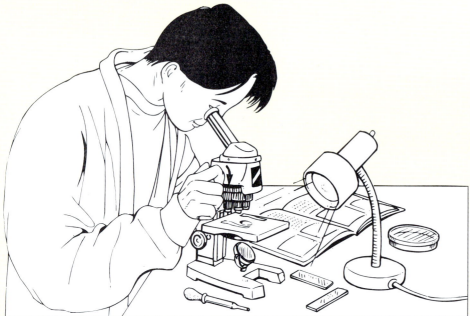

B Use a clean dropper. Add a drop of water to the slide. ▼

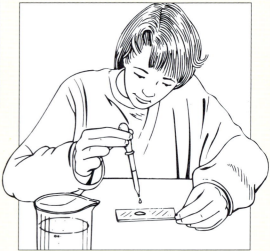

C Open the lid a little. Pick up some of the mould with the forceps. Close the lid. ◄

D Place the mould on the drop of water. Put the forceps in the beaker of water. ◄

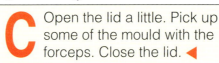

E Use the mounted needle. Carefully lower the coverslip on to your slide, try not to trap air bubbles. ▲

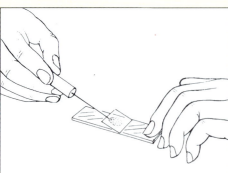

F Put your slide on to the stage of the microscope. Slowly turn the knob as shown until your slide is clearly seen in focus. ▲

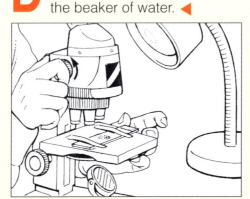

Q1 What does the mould look like in the dish?

Q2 Draw the mould as you saw it with the microscope. On your drawing label: 'Threads which grow and spread to get food', 'Black pin heads, which contain spores'.

Q3 Spores make up 50% of household dust. If they land on food they **germinate**. This means that they grow new threads. How do you think that spores get to new bread?

How do microbes cause food poisoning?

Some microbes make **toxins** (poisonous wastes) which make us ill. Toxins cause stomach pain, loss of appetite, sickness and diarrhoea. Absorption of nutrients is reduced. Drinking plenty of fluids, prevents harmful **dehydration** (loss of water). Usually we get better quickly. If microbes multiply in the food there will be more toxins. This makes us more seriously ill. Some microbes can cause death.

Types of food poisoning	Typical causes
Salmonella	Raw eggs and chicken from infected hens
Listeria	Soft cheeses and chilled foods left in the warmth
Botulism	Meat, vegetables and 'faulty' tins of food
Typhoid	People who are not ill but are **carriers** of germs
Cholera	Water from rivers, pumps or wells infected with sewage

Flies carry microbes. When they land they clean themselves. Flies have no teeth. They have to soften food using their saliva and liquid from their stomach. Flies suck most of this up. We eat all that they leave behind.

Microbes can come from dirty hands and dirty habits. Microbes will multiply in dirty, unhygienic kitchens. 'Carriers' should not work in kitchens.

Extension exercise 5 can be used now.

Q1 What makes us ill?

Q2 Why are flies dangerous?

Q3 How can we keep flies off food?

Q4 Why is food poisoning more common in the summer?

Q5 Your mum puts the uncooked chicken on top of some boiled ham in the fridge. Write down how you would explain to her that this is dangerous.

3 Working microbes

What is biotechnology?

▼ **Biotechnology** uses living **cells**. Cells can make things that we want. Many of the methods used in biotechnology today were first used thousands of years ago.

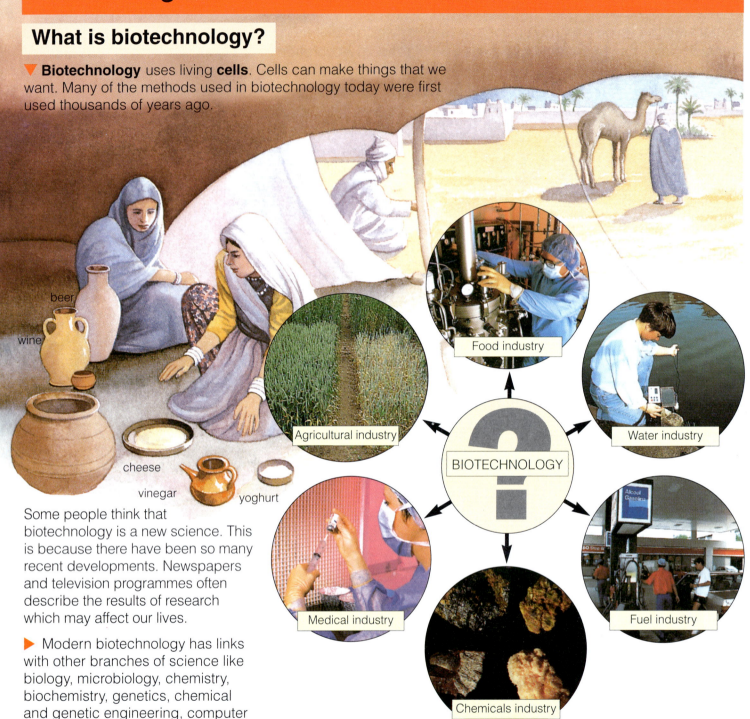

Some people think that biotechnology is a new science. This is because there have been so many recent developments. Newspapers and television programmes often describe the results of research which may affect our lives.

▶ Modern biotechnology has links with other branches of science like biology, microbiology, chemistry, biochemistry, genetics, chemical and genetic engineering, computer science and environmental science.

Q1 What is biotechnology?

Q2 What are some of the products of the oldest biotechnology processes?

Q3 Modern biotechnology can be divided into several main areas of study. What are these areas?

Q4 Why do people think that biotechnology is a new science?

3 Working microbes

What are enzymes?

Enzymes control chemical reactions. They can build or break down substances. In this experiment, you are going to find out how heat affects the work of the enzyme **amylase**.

Apparatus

- [ ] starch solution [ ] water
- [ ] amylase solution [ ] tripod
- [ ] boiled amylase solution
- [ ] 5 test tubes [ ] heatproof mat
- [ ] dropper pipette [ ] gauze
- [ ] iodine solution [ ] stop clock
- [ ] 250 cm^3 beaker
- [ ] marker pen [ ] Bunsen burner
- [ ] test tube rack
- [ ] 10 cm^3 measuring cylinder
- [ ] 0–100°C thermometer
- [ ] eye protection

 Wear eye protection.

Q1 Copy this table.

Tube	Contents	Temperature	Colour with iodine solution after 20 minutes
1	10 cm^3 water	room	
2	10 cm^3 starch solution	room	
3	10 cm^3 starch solution	35°C	
4	10 cm^3 starch solution + 5 cm^3 amylase	35°C	
5	10 cm^3 starch solution + 5 cm^3 boiled amylase	35°C	

A Label the test tubes 1–5. Add 10 cm^3 water to tube 1. Add 10 cm^3 starch solution to tubes 2–5. ▲

B Half fill the beaker with water. Heat it until there is a steady temperature of 35°C.

C Add 5 cm^3 of amylase solution to tube 4. Add 5 cm^3 of boiled amylase solution to tube 5. Shake tubes 4 and 5 gently to mix the contents. Place tubes 3, 4 and 5 in the prepared beaker for 20 minutes. ▲

D Add 4 drops of iodine solution to test tubes 1–5. Record your results in your table. ◄

Q2 What colour is iodine solution when starch is present?

Q3 What colour is iodine solution when starch is absent?

Q4 Is starch solution destroyed, or changed, by heating it at 35–40°C? Explain your answer.

Q5 What does amylase do to starch? Explain your answer.

Q6 How is amylase affected by boiling?

Extension exercise 6 can be used now.

3 Working microbes

Living cells and enzymes

Hydrogen peroxide is a poison that can form in living cells. An enzyme called catalase can change it to harmless water and oxygen. In this experiment, you are going to find out how living things react with hydrogen peroxide.

1 Look carefully to see if any bubbles are produced.
2 If there are lots of bubbles test them with a glowing spill; it will relight if oxygen is present.
3 Measure the height of any froth or foam produced.

Apparatus

- apple ☐ potato ☐ meat
- liver ☐ hydrogen peroxide
- knife ☐ cutting tile
- 0–10 cm³ measuring cylinder
- Bunsen burner ☐ heatproof mat
- 2 wooden spills ☐ mm ruler
- 8 test tubes ☐ test tube rack
- eye protection

Wear eye protection.

Handle the hydrogen peroxide with care.

Q1 Copy this table.

Tube	Contents	Amount of bubbles	Test with glowing spill	Height of froth (mm)
①	apple			
②	chopped apple			

A Label the test tubes 1–8. Add 2 cm³ hydrogen peroxide to each tube. ▲

B Add a cube of apple to tube 1. Record your results in the table. ▲

C Chop up another cube of apple. Add the small pieces to tube 2. Record your results in the table. ▼

D Repeat **B** and **C** for potato, meat, and liver. Record your results after each test.

Q2 Which was best at changing hydrogen peroxide?

Q3 Which cells, plant or animal, worked the fastest?

Q4 Why do living cells break down hydrogen peroxide?

Q5 How do the cells break down hydrogen peroxide?

Q6 How did chopping up the apple, potato, and so on, alter the speed of the reaction? Explain why?

Extension exercise 7 can be used now.

3 Working microbes

Biological washing powders

Biological washing powders contain enzymes. The makers claim they are good at removing stains. In this experiment you are going to find out if this is really true.

Q1 Copy this table.

Cloth number	Stain	Appearance at first	Appearance after washing
1	coffee		
2	grass		
3	blackcurrant juice		
4	biro ink		
5	grease		
6	chocolate		

Apparatus

- 6 labelled containers of white cloth stained with: coffee, grass, blackcurrant juice, biro ink, grease, chocolate
- gauze
- biological washing powder
- spatula
- measuring cylinder
- large beaker
- stirrer
- waterproof marker pen
- Bunsen burner
- tripod
- stop clock
- heatproof mat
- 0–100°C thermometer
- eye protection
- forceps

Wear eye protection.

Some people are allergic to biological washing powders. Avoid contact with both powder and solution.

A Number each piece of cloth. Describe the appearance of the stain in your table. ▲

B Add 5 spatulas of washing powder to the large beaker. Add 150 cm³ water gradually, stirring until the powder is dissolved. Repeat these steps until the beaker is half full. Warm the water gently until it reaches 30°C. Turn the Bunsen out. ▲

C Add the pieces of cloth. Stir the contents of the beaker frequently. ▲

D After 15–20 minutes use forceps to remove each piece of cloth. Rinse each one in cold water. Let the cloth dry. Complete your results table. ▶

Q2 Which stains were removed best?

Q3 Which stains remained?

Q4 How do biological washing powders work?

Q5 What did your experiment show about the claims made for stain removal?

Q6 What, if any, were the warnings given about using biological washing powder?

Q7 Was your method of testing the washing powder fair? Could you get better results? Explain your answer.

3 Working microbes

A whiter wash?

In this experiment you are going to find out how biological washing powders compare with non-biological powders at different temperatures.

Q1 Copy this table.

Beaker	Temperature °C	Powder	Appearance of cloth at first	Appearance of cloth after washing
1	100 (very hot)	biological		
2	100 (very hot)	non-biological		
3	30 (warm)	biological		
4	30 (warm)	non-biological		

Apparatus

- 4 × 250 cm³ beakers
- spatula
- marker pen
- eye protection
- measuring cylinder
- stirrer
- 4 pieces of stained white cloth
- Bunsen burner
- tripod
- forceps
- gauze
- 0–100°C thermometer
- biological washing powder
- 4 heatproof mats
- stop clock
- non-biological washing powder

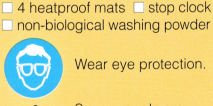

Wear eye protection.

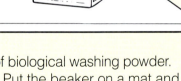

Some people are allergic to biological washing powders. Avoid contact with both powder and solution.

A Label the beakers 1, 2, 3 and 4. Add 150 cm³ water to each beaker. Complete the fourth column of the table. ▲

B Boil the water in beaker 1. Add 5 spatulas of biological washing powder. Stir until it dissolves. Add a piece of cloth. Put the beaker on a mat and leave for 15–20 minutes. Stir it often. Remove the cloth using forceps. Rinse it in cold water and let it dry. Record your results on the table. ▲

C Repeat **B** for beaker 2 but this time using the non-biological washing powder. Record your results. ▲

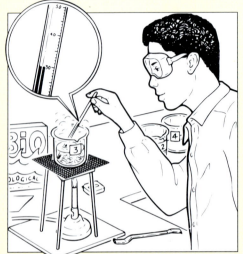

D Repeat **B** for beakers 3 and 4 using water at 30°C. Take care to use the correct powder. Complete your table. ▲

Q2 Which powder gave the best results in cool water?

Q3 Which powder gave the best results in the very hot water?

Q4 Why are the results affected by temperature?

Q5 If both powders cost the same, which would be the cheapest powder to use at home? Explain your answer.

3 Working microbes

Making yoghurt

People have made yoghurt for thousands of years. In hot countries it was a good way to preserve milk. Today you are going to make yoghurt.

Q1 Copy this table.

Beaker	Contents	Appearance of contents after 1–2 days
X	milk and boiled yoghurt	
Y	milk and unboiled yoghurt	

Apparatus

- ☐ teaspoon ☐ eye protection ☐ stirrer
- ☐ natural live yoghurt ☐ heatproof mat
- ☐ 2 × 250 cm³ beakers ☐ gauze
- ☐ marker pen ☐ clingfilm ☐ tripod
- ☐ UHT milk ☐ Bunsen burner

 Wear eye protection.

 Do not taste the yoghurt you make.

A Label 2 beakers X and Y. Put 3 teaspoons of yoghurt into each one. Gently heat beaker X. Stir until it boils. Leave it to cool. ▲

B Add milk to half fill beaker X and stir it. Repeat this step for beaker Y. Cover each beaker and keep them warm for 24 hours. Then keep them in a fridge for 1–2 days. Observe and record the results. ▲

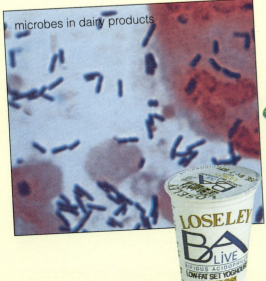
microbes in dairy products

Q2 Why was yoghurt made?

Q3 What could have been destroyed by boiling?

Q4 Why do you think that the beakers had to be covered?

Q5 Which beaker produced a substance most like yoghurt?

Q6 What do you think changes milk to yoghurt?

3 Working microbes

Making cheese

In this experiment you are going to find out how to turn milk into cheese.

Apparatus

- ☐ 2 × 250 cm³ beakers
- ☐ 20 cm³ measuring cylinder
- ☐ 0–100°C thermometer
- ☐ Bunsen burner ☐ tripod
- ☐ gauze ☐ heatproof mat
- ☐ 2 filter funnels ☐ filter paper
- ☐ clingfilm ☐ lemon juice
- ☐ microbe culture ☐ marker pen
- ☐ pasteurised milk
- ☐ 2 small beakers
- ☐ eye protection

 Wear eye protection.

 Do not taste the cheese you make.

Beaker	Contents	Appearance				
		at start	after 15 minutes	after 1–2 days	solid left in filter paper	liquid passed through filter paper
①	milk and lemon juice					
②	milk and microbes					

A Label the beakers 1 and 2. Add 150 cm³ of milk to each beaker. Warm the milk in both beakers to 40°C. ▶

B Add 15 cm³ lemon juice to beaker 1 and stir. Make a note of the appearance in your table. Keep this beaker in a warm place for 15 minutes. Fill in the next part of your table. Filter the contents of the beaker. You may have to leave this until the next lesson before you can complete the table. ▲

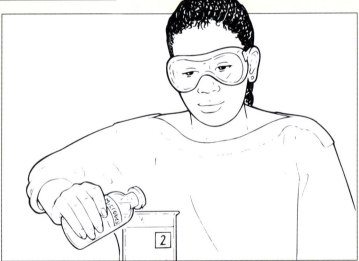

C Add the sample of microbes to beaker 2 and stir. Wash your hands! Make a note of the appearance in your table. Cover this beaker and keep it in a warm place for 1–2 days. Filter the contents of beaker 2 as in **B**. Complete the last sections of your table. ▲

Q2 What happened to the milk in beaker 1 after 15 minutes?

Q3 What sort of chemical is lemon juice?

Q4 What did the microbes do to the milk after 1–2 days?

Q5 What could the microbes have made to curdle the milk?

Q6 Which beaker made a solid which looked and smelt most like cheese?

Q7 How could the solid be changed to look like a hard cheese?

Extension exercise 8 can be used now.

3 Working microbes

Bread

Bread is made from wheat flour and **yeast**. Wheat has enzymes which change starch to sugar. Yeast is a fungus which feeds on sugar. Its enzymes break down the sugar in the flour. Carbon dioxide is made. This gas makes the dough rise. The dough is baked to make bread. You are going to find out how well yeast works.

Apparatus

- [ ] plain flour [ ] sugar
- [ ] top pan balance
- [ ] 250 cm^3 beaker
- [ ] 25 cm^3 measuring cylinder
- [ ] yeast solution [ ] stirrer
- [ ] 250 cm^3 measuring cylinder
- [ ] stop clock [ ] slice of bread

Q1 Copy this table.

Time (mins)	Volume (cm^3)
0 (start)	
2	
4	

A Weigh 20 g of flour and add it to the beaker. Then add 1 g sugar. ▼

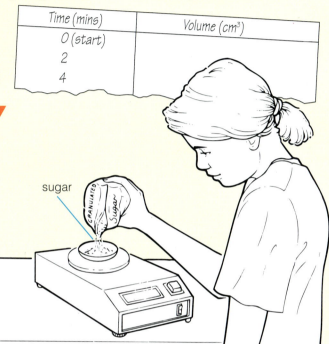

B Measure 25 cm^3 yeast solution. Add this to the contents of the beaker. Stir until it is smooth. ▼

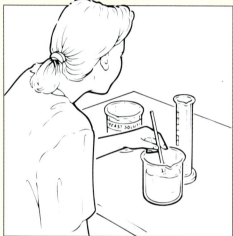

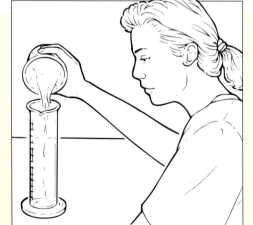

C Carefully pour the contents of the beaker into the 250 cm^3 measuring cylinder. *Do not* let the contents touch the sides! ▲

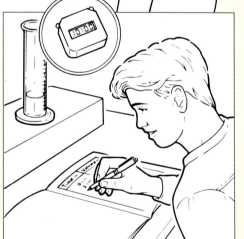

D Record the volume of the paste every 2 minutes for 30 minutes. ▲

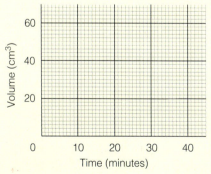

E Plot a line graph of your results. ▲

Q2 What made the dough rise?

Q3 Why was sugar added?

Q4 What does the yeast make to break down sugar?

Q5 What can you see in a slice of bread that shows that yeast produced a gas?

3 Working microbes

Fermentation

Yeast is often found on the surface of sweet fruits. In **fermentation** enzymes produced by yeast change sugar into carbon dioxide and alcohol. Carbon dioxide turns lime water cloudy. Alcohol has a special smell.

Q1 Copy this table.

	At start	After 1–2 weeks
colour of limewater		
appearance of juice		
smell of juice		

A Rinse all the apparatus in sterilising solution to kill all the microbes.

B Measure 100 cm³ apple juice into a flask. Add 4 cm³ yeast culture. Then add 6 cm³ distilled water. ▼

Apparatus

- apple juice
- yeast culture
- distilled water
- limewater
- 2 × 250 cm³ flasks
- 10 cm³ measuring cylinder
- 100 cm³ measuring cylinder
- 2 bungs with glass tubing and rubber connectors
- sterilising solution

Do not taste anything in the lab.

C Add enough limewater to the second flask so that the end of the glass tube will be in the liquid. ▲

Q2 What signs are there that changes are occurring in the first flask?

Q3 How do you know that the gas produced is carbon dioxide?

Q4 What do the contents of the flask smell like at the end of the experiment?

Q5 Apart from your age, why do you think that you are not allowed to taste what is in the flask?

Q6 Why do you think the yeast stops making carbon dioxide?

D Add the bungs and glass tubing as shown. Complete the second column of your table. Keep the flasks warm for 1–2 weeks. Complete your table. ▲

Extension exercise 9 can be used now.

3 Working microbes

Germinating maize

Germinating grains are used to make beer. Grains like maize (sweetcorn) contain starch. They need energy to **germinate** and grow. Sugar can provide energy. You are going to find out what happens when maize germinates.

Apparatus
- ☐ 2 sterile Petri dishes ☐ scalpel
- ☐ 2 tubes of melted starch agar
- ☐ marker pen ☐ 2 maize grains
- ☐ 2 boiled maize grains
- ☐ forceps ☐ dilute iodine solution
- ☐ cutting tile ☐ eye protection

Q1 Copy this table.

Final appearance	
① unboiled grain and starch agar	② boiled grain and starch agar

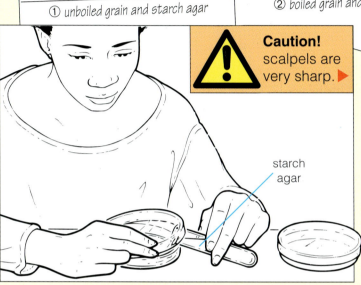

Caution! scalpels are very sharp.

starch agar

A Label the bottom of each dish with your name, date and dish number. Quickly pour the starch agar into each dish. Quickly replace their lids. Leave the dishes until the agar has set. ▲

B Cut each unboiled grain in half as shown. Using forceps place them, cut side down, on the agar of dish 1. Quickly replace the lid. Repeat using the boiled grains for dish 2. ▲

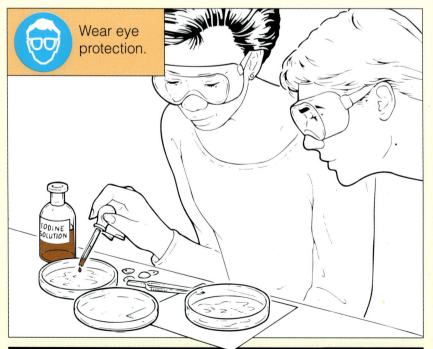

Wear eye protection.

C Leave the dishes in a warm place for 1–7 days. Remove the dish lids. Remove the grains with forceps. Add dilute iodine solution to cover the agar surface of each dish. After 1–2 minutes pour the liquid off. Look at the dishes over a white background. Record your results in the table. ◄

Q2 What is stored in grains?

Q3 What do the grains need for growth and germination?

Q4 Iodine solution turns blue-black with starch. What do your results show in dish 1?

Q5 What is the effect of boiling the grains?

Q6 How could the maize grains produce these results?

Extension exercise 10 can be used now.

3 Working microbes

Genetic engineering

Genes control the appearance, chemistry and behaviour of organisms. Genetic engineering involves finding, isolating and removing genes. It has helped people with diseases like diabetes.

Living things are made of cells. Large organisms like plants and animals are multicellular (many celled). Small organisms like bacteria are unicellular (single celled). All living cells have **DNA**. DNA controls cell development and chemical activity.

There are 46 chromosomes in the nucleus of a human cell. They are made of DNA and have special areas called genes. Genes control processes like protein production. Bacteria do not have a nucleus. Their genes are on a circular molecule of DNA. Some bacteria have a small separate loop of DNA called a **plasmid**. Plasmids can be transferred to other bacteria. They take their genes with them.

Genetic engineering often involves transferring genes from one species to another. Enzymes can be used to 'cut out' a single gene from DNA. This 'donor gene' can then be isolated. It can be joined into a plasmid using different enzymes. The plasmid acts as a carrier. It takes the donor gene into bacteria cells. Bacteria and their new gene can be **cloned** in a fermenter.

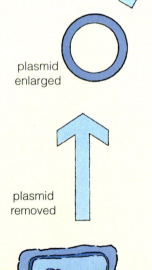

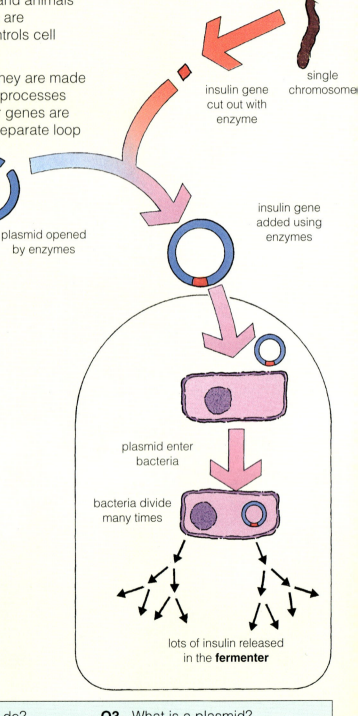

| Q1 What does DNA do? | Q3 What is a plasmid? |
| Q2 What do genes control? | Q4 What is genetic engineering? |

3 Working microbes

Helping people with diabetes

Part of our body called the **pancreas** makes the hormone **insulin**. Insulin is a protein which controls how much sugar there is in our blood. A person with too much or too little sugar in their blood goes into a **coma** (becomes unconscious). Some people have **diabetes**. Their pancreas cannot make enough insulin. Their blood sugar level is not controlled. Without insulin people die. In the past people were given insulin from cattle and pigs. It was difficult to get the amount needed and it was of poor quality and expensive.

Now genetic engineering has produced bacteria which can make insulin. Bacteria, with the donor gene for making insulin, are kept in a **fermenter**. Large quantities of insulin are soon made.

Insulin and bacteria are removed from the fermenter. They are easily separated. The insulin is tested for quality. It should be exactly the same as human insulin. The bacteria are checked and can be re-used. This reduces the cost of the process.

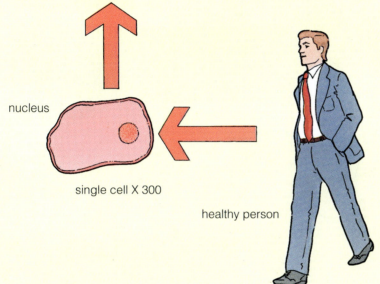

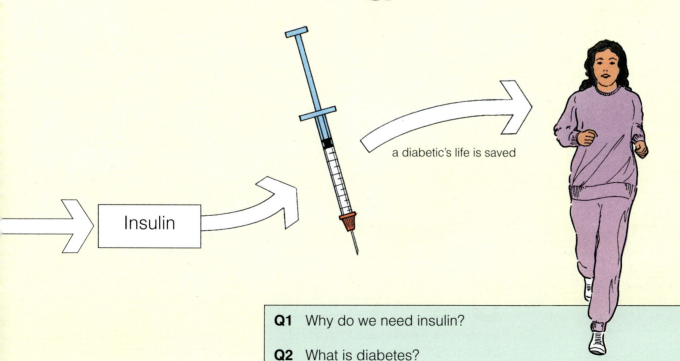

Q1 Why do we need insulin?

Q2 What is diabetes?

Q3 What are the advantages of using bacteria to produce insulin?

3 Working microbes

What can microbes break down?

Some things will rot if they are left in the garden. Anything which can be broken down by microbes is called **biodegradable**. See if you can find out which things are biodegradable.

Apparatus
- ☐ large container
- ☐ large beaker of water
- ☐ plastic gloves ☐ string
- ☐ 8 plastic labels
- ☐ polythene bag/cover
- ☐ fresh, fertile garden soil
- ☐ samples of: bread, a petal, a leaf, paper, plastic, tinfoil, polythene, biodegradable bag

Q1 Copy this table.

Sample	Appearance when fresh	Appearance after a month
Bread	White and...	

A Put half of the soil into the container. Use the water to make the soil damp. ▲

⚠ Always wash your hands after handling soil.

B Complete the first two columns of the table for each sample. Write a label for each sample. ▲

C Level the soil. Space out each sample on the surface. Mark each one with the correct label. ▲

D Cover the samples with the rest of the soil. Take care not to move the labels. Cover the container and leave it in a warm place for a month. Make sure it doesn't get dry.
After a month look at each sample (wear plastic gloves). Complete your table. ▲

Q2 What does biodegradable mean?

Q3 Which things are not biodegradable and did not change?

Q4 Which things changed the most?

Q5 Which things have started to change?

Q6 Microbes caused the changes. Where did they come from?

Q7 Why is it a good thing that biodegradable bags and packaging are now used?

3 Working microbes

Microbes and recycling

Green plants are the only living things that make their own food. All animals depend on plants. Plants make the oxygen that animals need for breathing. Animals eat the food made by the plants.

Plant foods contain **minerals** which were once in the soil. Minerals are needed for healthy growth.

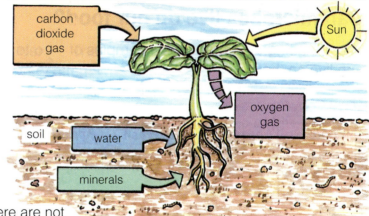

▼ Farming quickly removes minerals from the soil. If there are not enough minerals plants won't grow properly and may die. Farmers have learnt to add minerals back to the soil to get good crops.

▼ In natural environments animals do not remove as much food as farmers. Microbes in the soil will cause all the plant and animal remains to rot. In this way minerals are returned to the soil. This is called **recycling**.

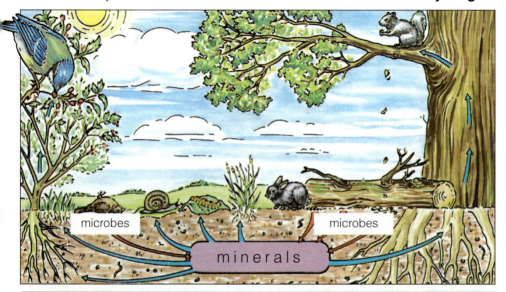

Q1 What do plants provide for animals?

Q2 What do green plants need to make their food?

Q3 What plant foods do you eat? (**Hint**: think about the foods you see in the supermarket.)

Q4 What happens to plants if there are not enough minerals in the soil?

Q5 Why isn't there a shortage of minerals in the soil?

Q6 What would our environment look like if microbes did not cause rotting?

Extension exercise 11 can be used now.

31

3 Working microbes

Sewage disposal

Dirty water is collected from our homes and factories in underground pipes called **sewers**. In Britain 400 litres of **sewage** are produced per person each day. This is because so much water is used in factories and homes. Diseases like cholera, polio, gastric 'flu and food poisoning can be passed on by infected sewage. Poisonous wastes in the water from factories could damage the environment. It is important that sewage is made safe to protect our health and our environment.

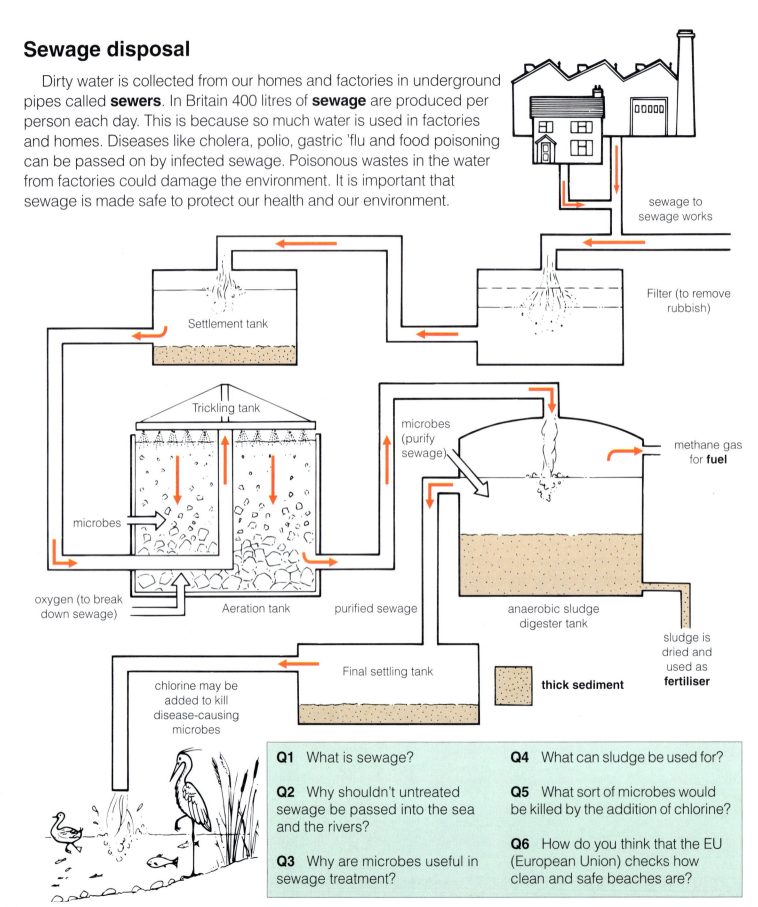

Q1 What is sewage?

Q2 Why shouldn't untreated sewage be passed into the sea and the rivers?

Q3 Why are microbes useful in sewage treatment?

Q4 What can sludge be used for?

Q5 What sort of microbes would be killed by the addition of chlorine?

Q6 How do you think that the EU (European Union) checks how clean and safe beaches are?